Adult Family Homes

*A Commentary on Applying the
Building Codes in WA State*

John P Neff, CBO

Code Central Consulting

authorHOUSE®

AuthorHouse™
1663 Liberty Drive
Bloomington, IN 47403
www.authorhouse.com
Phone: 1-800-839-8640

First published by AuthorHouse 5/10/2011

ISBN: 978-1-4567-5692-5 (e)
ISBN: 978-1-4567-5299-6 (sc)

Library of Congress Control Number: 2011904391

Printed in the United States of America

Any people depicted in stock imagery provided by Thinkstock are models,
and such images are being used for illustrative purposes only.
Certain stock imagery © Thinkstock.

This book is printed on acid-free paper.

Dedicated to those State AFH Licensors and the Providers who make the lives of the elderly in WA State so much easier—and to those building code officials who understand their needs and assist in their better living experience in an Adult Family Home!

ACKNOWLEDGMENTS

This book could not have been created without
the help of Casey Zimmer, RN and Gary Allsup,
Building Code Specialist and my wife, Joanie.

Further, all graphics showing the installation requirements
were created Jeff L. Eberle, Certified Professional Building
Designer, and owner of The Eberle Brothers, LLC, Olympia,
WA.   Jeff has granted the reprint of his drawings in this
book, for which I thank him!

jpn

FOREWORD

Adult Family Homes (AFH) are an important part of care-giving for elderly persons at specific times in their lives. We know that no one chooses to move from their own home into a care facility. When they do, they deserve the safest and most caring environment they can possibly receive. It is very important for the local code officials to do everything they can to serve those specific needs.

We hope the use of this handbook as your field guide will provide the best practices to meet the needs of the AFH resident. Suggested alternate methods shown in the booklet were developed in cooperation with DSHS licensors.

Contents

Chapter One

Purpose of this Document

This document was written to provide care providers and inspectors an easy-to-follow guide to the code for Adult Family Homes. The issues of ramps, stairs, handrails, access, grab bars and smoke alarms are covered in this guide in a manner that makes it easier to follow and comply. While the code contains accessibility requirements for each of these items, we know that those were written for all types of people—with all types of disabilities, not just elderly persons.

This book was written to provide local code officials with good examples that will work for the residents living within Adult Family Homes. It also is intended to give code officials confidence in approving alternative methods by using these examples.

We concluded, after talking with care-givers, that strict compliance with the letter of the code is not in the best interests of the elderly residents, but compliance with approval of alternate methods is in their interest.

CHAPTER TWO

ADA—A COMPARISON WITH THE NEEDS OF THE ELDERLY

The Americans with Disabilities Act (ADA) was developed for use in "places of public accommodation" and was developed for a wide-ranging scope of persons with disabilities. The Act addresses the specific construction and employment provisions for anyone with qualified disabilities—the elderly being but one subset of this population.

The ADA Accessibility Guidelines does not typically apply in private homes, as noted in the "ADA Q&A" from the US Department of Justice: *"The ADA does not cover strictly residential private apartments and homes. If, however, a place of public accommodation, such as a doctor's office or day care center, is located in a private residence, those portions of the residence used for that purpose are subject to the ADA's requirements."* And, the Guidelines address typical commercial-type uses, where the public goes for service or various activities.

NEEDS OF THE ELDERLY ARE DIFFERENT

Further, the people envisioned for the ADA Guidelines are any age of person with any disability that affects a "major life function." While the elderly may have those types of disabilities that affect a major life function, the specific needs of the elderly in a private home care setting are far different that the broad brush used in development of ADA Guidelines.

CHAPTER THREE

WHAT IS THE <u>REAL</u> NEED?

The purpose of this book is to provide code officials, State AFH licensing employees and AFH providers guidelines for applying the accessibility items, including the grab bar requirements in WA State IRC Section R325 for Adult Family Homes. It is also meant to provide a way to approve "alternate methods" for grab bars in AFH residences. It is also written to provide an assurance that the approved grab bars meet the intent of the code as written; and provide the residents with the appropriate grab bars to allow them confidence in their safety in the home.

In developing this book, the author, in cooperation with providers and licensors examined the needs of the elderly in the home. We also looked at the needs in the bathroom for the use of grab bars at the toilet and in showers, bathtubs and combination units. It is very clear that the specific needs of the elderly are not addressed well enough in the ADA to be appropriate to AFH.

Toilet Grab Bars:

The biggest problem the elderly face in toileting is that their upper thigh strength--and to a lesser degree, upper arm strength--has generally been lost. That makes it difficult to sit down on any lower surface, be it a typical chair, couch, or toilet. Because of this, there is a need to have a grab bar on both sides of a toilet. Typically, they use the horizontal grab bars on each side to slow their descent, as they start to sit and then have to "fall" into place. Using those grab bars allows them to slow that sitting action and it prevents them from falling to one side or the other.

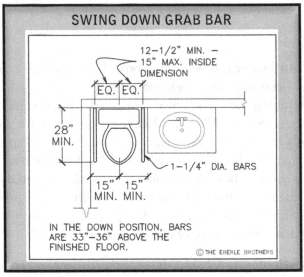

For toilets, we found that the best grab bars are those that—while being listed as holding the 250-pound force requirement in the ADA, in both the grab bar itself and the connection to the wall—are those that can be lifted up against the wall as needed. (See chapter 4 for attachment and dimension examples.)

Tub/Shower Combination Bathing Units

The need for grab bars in the typical fiberglass tub/shower units is not solved by following the ADA /ANSI standards. The needs of the elderly are different than the "answers" provided by the ADA or ANSI Standards.

For a tub/shower combination unit, since the resident may or may not sit on a shower bench in the unit, it is best to install grab bars as illustrated in chapter 4. Remember, in this case, the resident needs to step up over the bath tub front side which is typically about 18 inches tall. That is almost always a problem, as their upper leg strength has gradually declined over the years.

There should be an 18 inch vertical grab bar installed at each corner to enter the tub.

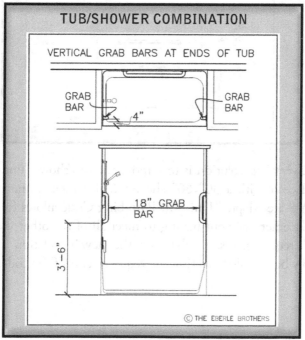

Once into the unit, the resident needs a horizontal grab bar at 33-36 inches above the bottom of the tub unit. The 24 inch minimum bar should start 12 inches from the valve (faucet) end, leaving 24 inches at the other end opposite of the valve/faucet.

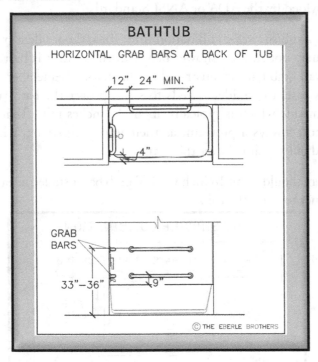

The very best solution is to remove the tub/shower unit and replace it with a 30"x60" shower replacement unit. (The WA State-adopted Uniform Plumbing Code allows for this replacement without having to meet all of the other shower code requirements. Grab bars in the "new installation" could easily be installed meeting the requirements of the code.

Stand-up Showers

In a shower stall, install an 18" vertical grab bar at each exterior corner of the shower. Install the vertical bars on the outside wall of the unit, a minimum of 3 inches and maximum of 6 inches above the interior valve end horizontal grab bar. This gives the resident confidence getting into and out of the shower unit.

Inside the stall, install a horizontal grab bar at the side with the shower valve. Install another grab bar on the back wall opposite the door/opening into the shower. Both of these grab bars must be installed at 33-36 inches above the floor surface of the shower.

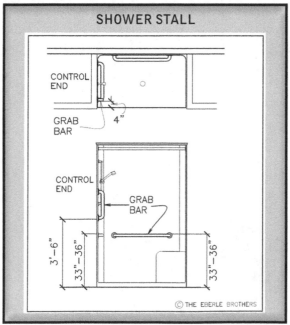

After the home is licensed by DSHS, if there are even more specific needs for a particular resident, it is the responsibility of the AFH provider to meet that need.

CHAPTER FOUR

SPECIFIC DIMENSION ISSUES

The biggest issue created by strict compliance with the ADA/ANSI Standards for grab bars in AFH is the dimension requirements. The dimensions in the following illustrations are appropriate, as we discovered in our research with the licensors and providers.

BUT, remember, any grab bar installed must:

1) Meet the cross section dimensional measurement (**1.25" min, 2" max**) [ANSI 609.2.1.].

2) Bars and mounting also need to meet required structural strength (**250 lbs**) [ANSI 609.8.].

Toilets:

There should be 18" from the center of the toilet to the nearest wall. This would then allow the requirement of 15" from the grab bar to the center of the toilet to be met. In most residences, this will never work, as the toilet compartment is 30" in total width.

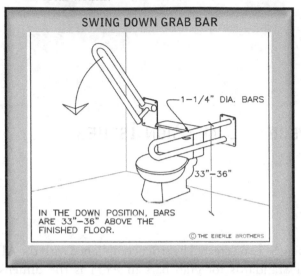

SWING DOWN GRAB BAR

1-1/4" DIA. BARS

33"-36"

IN THE DOWN POSITION, BARS ARE 33"-36" ABOVE THE FINISHED FLOOR.

© THE EBERLE BROTHERS

(A swing-up grab bar provides an approvable, alternate solution.)

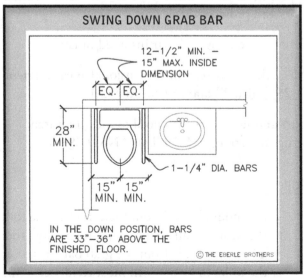

SWING DOWN GRAB BAR

12-1/2" MIN. – 15" MAX. INSIDE DIMENSION

EQ. EQ.

28" MIN.

1-1/4" DIA. BARS

15" 15" MIN. MIN.

IN THE DOWN POSITION, BARS ARE 33"-36" ABOVE THE FINISHED FLOOR.

© THE EBERLE BROTHERS

Tub/Shower Combinations:

In the tub/shower unit, the ADA/ANSI requirements also do not address the specific needs of the elderly in AFH. Once in the tub/shower unit, the resident should not be required to reach "down" to reach a grab bar. Remember, they already have very weak legs.

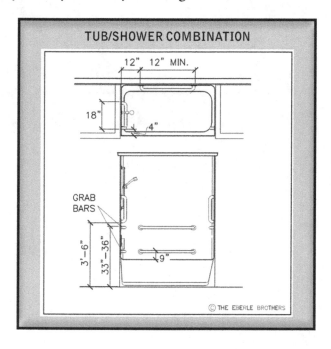

CHAPTER FIVE

ENTRY TO THE HOME

As you drove to the site of the AFH, were the *address numbers* clearly visible from the street? Does the site have an excessively long driveway preventing the house numbers from being visible from the street? Police, fire and emergency responders must be able to readily find the structure to render aid and assistance.

House numbers must be a minimum of 4 inches high and have a minimum of ½ inch stroke. Numbers must also be applied upon a contrasting background. If the house numbers are not visible from the street, additional numbering is necessary at the driveway entrance from the street.

Did you observe *fire hydrants* at the street? AFH's must have adequate fire access roads and a water supply meeting the local jurisdiction's requirements. *(Also see Chapter 8 on Fire Apparatus Access.)*

As you approach the main entry, is the sidewalk grade smooth and consistent without any differential settlement?

Remember the elderly residents, because of loss of leg muscle strength, tend to shuffle their feet so any small change in elevation is a potential trip hazard. Any elevation differential along the walkway greater than ¼ inch must be addressed per DSHS licensing requirements.

Classification Based on Steps:

The "classification" of the sleeping rooms for AFH residents relates only to the level of ambulation required for those residents. The type of entry(ies) to the home determines the sleeping rooms classifications. So, the entry--whether it needs a ramp or not--is very important.

Type S: There are steps/stairs in the access way to the bedroom. Those stairs can be outside the front door of the home, the steps across a sunken area inside the house that has to be crossed to get to the bedrooms, or a staircase inside the home reaching a bedroom on a second story, for example. Anytime there is even one step to get into the home or to a bedroom, the sleeping rooms are to be classified as Type S.

Type NS1: This classification means that there are no steps at one of the access ways/doors into the home and no steps inside that affect the access to a bedroom. For example, there may be steps at the main front door, but there is an at-grade entry at the other door into the home.

Type NS2: This means that there are no steps at any entrance into the home and no steps inside that affect the access to a bedroom.

Remember, to be a legal egress door, the door must be a

side hinged door with a minimum width of 32 inches. (See 2009 IRC R311.2)

A patio sliding door does not qualify as an exit.

Does the exit provide egress to a safe location of adequate distance from the structure in the event of a fire?

Now that you have determined the classification of the sleeping rooms based upon your observations, do you have steps, a ramp or is the entry at grade level serving this home?

- At-grade entries in typical homes—according to the IRC--may have a threshold up to 1 ½ inches in height above the walking surface. Thresholds exceeding the 1 ½" maximum then should be treated as a ramp on both sides of the threshold as described in Chapter 9 of this booklet.

  However, a threshold of this height is a tripping hazard and does not allow a walker or wheelchair to enter with minimal effort. Even though allowed by the code for homes, this height of threshold should not be used. A threshold ramp should be placed on each side of such a threshold to provide a smooth, easy-to-transition walking surface.

THRESHOLD RAMP

MAXIMUM SLOPE OF RAMP
FOR MAX. HT 1-1/2" THRESHOLDS:
1 VERTICAL TO 12 HORIZONTAL
1-1/2" THRESHOLD = 18" LENGTH

NOTE: The sloped ends of the threshold ramp are a risk for turning an ankle. Make the threshold ramp longer, to get the sloped end away from the walking path.

- If your entrance has steps, does the rise and run meet the requirement of a minimum 10 inch tread and a maximum rise of 7 ¾ inches?

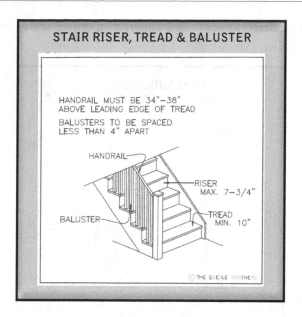

STAIR RISER, TREAD & BALUSTER

HANDRAIL MUST BE 34"–38"
ABOVE LEADING EDGE OF TREAD

BALUSTERS TO BE SPACED
LESS THAN 4" APART

HANDRAIL

RISER
MAX. 7-3/4"

BALUSTER

TREAD
MIN. 10"

© THE EHERLE BROTHERS

- Older homes (pre 2004) may have 9 inch treads and 8 inch risers. ALL steps—from one step to multiple steps--will need a handrail on both sides. (*See Chapter 9, Ramps and Handrails for specific requirements for the handrails. They are the same as for ramps.*)

- If your entrance has a ramp, **see Chapter 9, Ramps and Handrails.**

- Observe the main entry/exit door lockset. Does it have lever type handles?

- When activated from the inside does it completely unlock the mechanism? Secondary locking devices such as an independent deadbolt are not allowed. (See 2009 IRC R325.4)

To best comply with the requirements for the entry/exit

door latchset, look at the following example of a mortise-type lock:

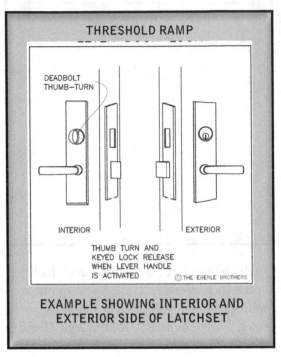

Note: the other side may have a thumb-turn to activate the deadbolt, as long as the lever handle on the inside retracts both the door strike and the deadbolt.

CHAPTER SIX

THE SLEEPING ROOM

Classification

The "classification" of the sleeping rooms for AFH residents relates only to the level of ambulation required for those residents. All sleeping rooms have to be classified as:

Type S:

Type NS1:

Type NS2:

[Refer to page 16 for specific requirements for each classification.]

Remember, you classify each sleeping room separately. You may have at least two of the classifications within the same home.

Types of Locking Devices within the Bedroom

Every bedroom door has to be openable from the outside of the room by the AFH provider in case it gets locked from the inside and the resident needs immediate assistance.

Every closet door has to be readily openable from the inside of the closet. Remember, that even with bypassing, sliding doors, there needs to be some type of opening hardware to allow a resident that may get into the closet and close the door to be able to get their fingers into the hardware to start the door moving.

All bedroom door hardware needs to be lever hardware.

Escape Windows and Doors

Every bedroom needs to have either a window or a door directly to the outside of the home to allow for emergency rescue or escape. If a door is provided, it needs lever hardware, and a single locking latch that only requires movement of the lever to unlock the door just like the main entry/exit door.

If there is not a door directly to the outside of the home, there must be a window meeting the following requirements:

> The <u>minimum</u> width of the opening (when opened fully) has to be at least 20 inches;

> The <u>minimum</u> height of the opening (when opened fully) has to be at least 24 inches.

But, the entire net opening (when fully opened) has to be at least 5.7 square feet in area (actual width X actual height = 5.7 or more).

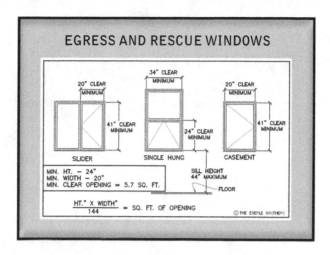

Smoke Detectors (Alarms)

See Chapter 7 for requirements for smoke detectors within bedrooms and the rest of the home.

CHAPTER SEVEN

SMOKE DETECTORS AND AUDIBILITY IN ADULT FAMILY HOMES

All Adult Family Homes must have smoke alarms installed as required in IRC Section R314. Alarms must be installed so that the fire warning may be audible in all parts of the dwelling upon activation of a single device.

All smoke alarms must be listed in accordance with UL 217, and installed in accordance with the provisions of this code.

(Household fire alarm systems installed in accordance with NFPA 72 that include smoke alarms, or a combination of smoke detector and audible notification device installed as required by this section for smoke alarms, shall be permitted.)

Location of Smoke Alarms

In Adult Family Homes, smoke alarms must be installed in the following locations:

1. In each resident sleeping room.

2. Outside each separate sleeping area in the immediate vicinity of the bedrooms.

3. On each additional story of the dwelling, including basements (but not including crawl spaces and uninhabitable attics). In dwellings or dwelling units with split levels and without an intervening door between the adjacent levels, a smoke alarm installed on the upper level shall be adequate for the adjacent lower level provided that the lower level is less than one full story below the upper level.

Since more than one smoke alarm is required to be installed within an Adult Family Home, the alarm devices must be interconnected so that the actuation of one alarm will activate all of the alarms. *There will be extremely few times only one is required.*

Power Source for Smoke Alarms

Smoke alarms must receive their primary power from the building wiring when such wiring is served from a commercial source (the local electrical utility company). When the primary power is interrupted, the smoke alarm must receive power from a battery. Wiring must be permanent and without a disconnecting switch other than the circuit breaker in the electrical panel.

Exceptions:

1) Smoke alarms may be battery-operated when installed in buildings without commercial power. *Note: DSHS will most likely not license an Adult Family Home if there is no commercial power served by an electric utility. See Chapter 12 for requirements of WAC 388-76.*

2) Battery-operated detectors and those that are not interconnected are allowed in existing areas of a home where the alterations or repairs do not result in the removal of interior wall or ceiling finishes exposing the structure (the framing of the house).

> HOWEVER, NOTE: If there is an attic, crawl space or basement which could provide access for hard wiring and interconnection without the removal of interior finishes, they must be interconnected.
>
> *In easier terms, if you can interconnect them through the attic, crawl space or basement, there is no exception to the requirement for interconnection.*

Remember the rule at the top of this chapter that says that the activation of a fire alarm shall be heard in all parts of the building? If the detectors are not interconnected, there must be a method of providing the alarm in the furthest part of the house away from the activating smoke alarm. For example, if the bedrooms are at one end of the home, and the laundry area is in the basement of the other end of the home, an alarm inside one of the bedrooms has to be able to be heard in the laundry area. That will be difficult without interconnection—or installing wireless, interconnecting smoke alarms.

CHAPTER 8

FIRE APPARATUS ACCESS ROADS AND WATER SUPPLY FOR FIRE PROTECTION

Note: The term "fire apparatus" means, in most communities, as "a vehicle such as a fire pumper, aerial ladder truck, fire tender, elevated platform, rescue squad, fire ground support vehicle, Medic One vehicle, ambulance, or similar firefighting equipment, including emergency medical response vehicles."

Adult Family Homes must be served by fire apparatus access roads and water supplies meeting the requirements of the local jurisdiction.

So, why is this in the code for Adult Family Homes? Because most Adult Family Homes are more frequent users of emergency medical and/or fire aid. Because of that frequency of use, the local fire code official needs to be contacted to verify access if there is any question at all about the location of the proposed Adult Family Home.

The basic rules are that the access roadway needs to be at

least 20 feet in width, unobstructed, and have an all-weather surface. If there are any bridges or bridge-like crossings in the access roadway, you must contact the fire code official to see if that bridge or crossing is approved for fire apparatus access.

CHAPTER 9

RAMPS & HANDRAILS

Slope:

All interior and exterior ramps, when provided, shall be constructed with a maximum slope of 1 vertical to 12 horizontal. As an example for figuring that slope; if the height the ramp needs to rise is 1-foot, the length of the ramp will need to be at least 12-feet long. If the rise needed is 18" (1-1/2-foot), the length of the ramp will need to be 18-feet long.

Note: The exception to meeting that requirement in the IRC, (of being technically infeasible to meet that slope) is not allowed for Adult Family Homes. There is never an exception to the slope requirement in Adult Family Homes.

Remember—any sidewalk or other walkway in the access to the home that <u>exceeds</u> the slope of 1 vertical to 20 horizontal is a ramp and be provided with the handrails, as noted next.

Handrails for Ramps

Handrails shall be installed on <u>both</u> sides of ramps between the slope of 1 vertical to 12 horizontal (maximum slope for a ramp) and 1 vertical and 20 horizontal (the slope at which a walkway becomes, by definition, a ramp) in accordance with R311.6.3.1 through R311.6.3.3.

Height of Handrails

The handrails must be between 34 inches and 38 inches above the surface of the ramp slope.

Grip Size

The handrails need to provide the ability to be grasped, and meet one of the following requirements:

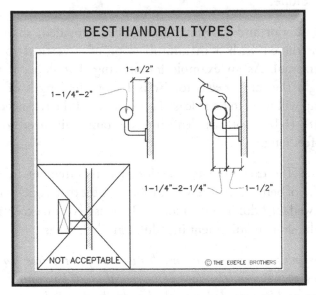

(One example of a grippable handrail. It must fit a person's hand and their ability to grip the hand-grip portion.)

(Second example of a handrail that is grippable. It has a spot for their fingers and their thumb to allow the grip on the handrail.)

Continuity of the Handrails

The handrails have to be continuous for the full length of the ramp. The ends have to be returned or have to terminate in a safety terminal. That is to prevent a sleeve of a coat from catching on the end of a hand rail.

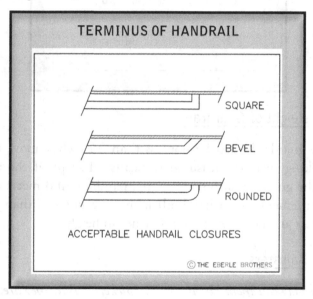

Guard(rail) for Ramps

Every ramp requires a handrail on each side, as already discussed. A ramp must have a guardrail on the open side(s) when the ramp is over 30 inches above the surrounding ground. (The guardrail is the portion below the handrail, that keeps a person, including children, from falling from the ramp. It includes the balusters, as described below.)

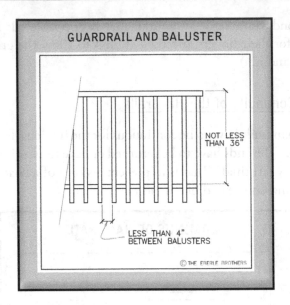

Height of Guardrail:

The guardrail must be not less than 36 inches above the walking surface, measured vertically. Except, if the top of the guardrail also serves as the handrail (and meets the requirements for a handrail) it may be not less than 34 inches and not more than 38 inches in height.

Balusters:

You may call them "banisters" or "pickets." But, they are the vertical members in a guardrail to prevent people—including children—from falling through.

Whatever you call them, they have to be spaced so a 4 inch sphere CANNOT pass between them, or pass between the bottom of the guardrail and the walking surface. The easiest method for meeting this requirement is to just have <u>less than</u> 4 inches between each of them!

Landings:

There has to be a landing at the top of a ramp and at any corner it turns. The Residential Code does not address landings in ramps where there is a need to provide accessibility to the elderly or others with disabilities. The code requires only a 36" landing, but that will not work either at a corner of a ramp, or at the top.

At the corner, a 36" x 36" landing is not large enough to get a large walker or a wheelchair around. The minimum dimensions the landing should be are 60" x 60".

At the top of a landing, there needs to be enough room to stop with a walker or a wheelchair, having the entire device (and person) at the level surface. If the landing is only 36" in length, the risk of rolling backwards, or falling backwards is likely. So, the landing at the top of a ramp also needs to be at least 60" long, in the direction of travel.

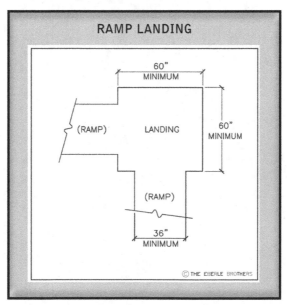

CHAPTER TEN

CARBON MONOXIDE ALARMS

The International Residential Code, as amended by the State Building Code Council requires carbon monoxide (CO) alarms in all homes.

Newly-built adult family homes require an approved carbon monoxide alarm must be installed outside of each separate sleeping area in the immediate vicinity of the bedroom(s).

In all other adult family homes, including existing homes being converted to an adult family home, they need the carbon monoxide alarms on and after July 1, 2011.

In existing homes, the CO alarms need to be installed the same as is required for new homes.

Alarm Requirements:

Single station carbon monoxide alarms shall be listed as complying with UL 2034 and shall be installed in accordance with this code and the manufacturer's installation instructions.

Buy only CO detectors with the notation of being listed in accordance with UL 2034.

CHAPTER ELEVEN

WAC 51-51-0325

Note: This is the International Residential Code (IRC) Section for Adult Family Homes (WAC 51-51-0325). It is inserted here so the reader will have the exact code language available.

SECTION R325
ADULT FAMILY HOMES

R325.1 General. This section shall apply to all newly constructed Adult Family Homes and all existing single family homes being converted to Adult Family Homes. This section shall not apply to those Adult Family Homes licensed by the state of Washington department of social and health services prior to July 1, 2001.

R325.2 Submittal Standards. In addition to those requirements in Section 106.1, the submittal shall identify the project as a Group R-3 Adult Family Home Occupancy. A floor plan shall be submitted identifying the means of egress and the components in the means of egress such as stairs, ramps, platform lifts and elevators. The plans shall indicate the rooms used for clients and the sleeping room classification of each room.

R325.3 Sleeping Room Classification. Each sleeping room in an Adult Family Home shall be classified as:

1. Type S - where the means of egress contains stairs, elevators or platform lifts.

2. Type NS1 - where one means of egress is at grade level or a ramp constructed in accordance with R325.9 is provided.

3. Type NS2 - where two means of egress are at grade level or ramps constructed in accordance with R325.9 are provided.

R325.4 Types of Locking Devices. All bedroom and bathroom doors shall be openable from the outside when locked.

Every closet shall be readily openable from the inside.

Operable parts of door handles, pulls, latches, locks and other devices installed in Adult Family Homes shall be operable with one hand and shall not require tight grasping, pinching or twisting of the wrist. The force required to activate operable parts shall be 5.0 pounds (22.2 N) maximum. Exit doors shall have no additional locking devices.

R325.5 Smoke Alarm Requirements. All Adult Family Homes shall be equipped with smoke alarms installed as required in Section R314. Alarms shall be installed in such a manner so that the fire warning may be audible in all parts of the dwelling upon activation of a single device.

R325.6 Escape Windows and Doors. Every sleeping room shall be provided with emergency escape and rescue windows as required by Section R310. No alternatives to the sill height such as steps, raised platforms or other devices placed by the openings will be approved as meeting this requirement.

R325.7 Fire Apparatus Access Roads and Water Supply for Fire Protection. Adult Family Homes shall be served by fire apparatus access roads and water supplies meeting the requirements of the local jurisdiction.

R325.8 Grab Bars. Grab bars shall be installed for all water closets and bathtubs and showers. The grab bars shall comply with ICC/ANSI A117.1 Sections 604.5 and 607.4 and 608.3.

> EXCEPTION:
> Grab bars are not required for water closets and bathtubs and showers used exclusively by staff of the Adult Family Home.

R325.9 Ramps. All interior and exterior ramps, when provided, shall be constructed in accordance with Section R311.8 with a maximum slope of 1 vertical to 12 horizontal. The exception to R311.8.1 is not allowed for Adult Family Homes. Handrails shall be installed in accordance with R325.9.1.

R325.9.1 Handrails for Ramps. Handrails shall be installed on both sides of ramps between the slope of 1 vertical to 12 horizontal and 1 vertical and 20 horizontal in accordance with R311.6.3.1 through R311.6.3.3.

R325.10 Stair Treads and Risers. Stair treads and risers shall be constructed in accordance with R311.7.4. Handrails shall be installed in accordance with R325.10.1.

R325.10.1 Handrails for Treads and Risers. Handrails shall be installed on both sides of treads and risers numbering from one riser to multiple risers. Handrails shall be installed in accordance with R311.7.7 through R311.7.7.4.

[Statutory Authority: Chapter 19.27 RCW. 10-18-036, § 51-51-0325, filed 8/25/10, effective 9/25/10. Statutory Authority: RCW 19.27.190, 19.27.020, and chapters 19.27 and 34.05 RCW. 09-04-023, § 51-51-0325, filed 1/27/09, effective 7/1/10. Statutory Authority: RCW 19.27.074, 19.27.020, and chapters 19.27 and 34.05 RCW. 07-01-090, § 51-51-0325, filed 12/19/06, effective 7/1/07. Statutory Authority: RCW 19.27.031 and 19.27.074. 04-01-109, § 51-51-0325, filed 12/17/03, effective 7/1/04.]

CHAPTER TWELVE

DSHS RULES

Note: This is the set of DSHS rules (WAC 388-76-10685 through 10810). It is inserted here so the reader will have the exact rules available.

WAC 388-76-10685 Through -10810. PHYSICAL PLANT BASIC REQUIREMENTS

388-76-10685
Bedrooms.

The Adult Family Home must:

1) Ensure each resident's bedroom is an outside room, which allows entrance of natural light;

2) Ensure window and door screens:

   a) Do not hinder emergency escape; and

   b) Prevent entrance of flies and other insects.

3) Ensure each resident, including those using mobility aids such as wheelchairs and walkers has direct, unrestricted, and free access from the bedroom through doors, hallways and corridors to common use areas and other rooms used for care and services including bathrooms;

4) Make separate bedrooms available for each sex;

5) Make reasonable efforts to accommodate residents wanting to share the room;

6) Provide each bedroom with a minimum usable floor space as required in WAC 388-76-10690.

7) Ensure each bedroom has a closet or a wardrobe, armoire or reasonable facsimile thereof. Neither the closet nor wardrobe/armoire floor space will be considered a part of the room's usable square footage. The home must not remove a closet in order to provide additional floor space.

8) Ensure no more than two residents to a bedroom;

9) Unless the resident chooses to provide their own furniture and bedding, the home must provide each resident a bed thirty-six inches or more wide with:

   a) A clean, comfortable mattress;

   b) A waterproof cover for use when needed or requested by the resident;

   c) Clean sheets and pillow cases;

d) Adequate clean blankets to meet the needs of each resident; and

e) Clean pillows.

10) Not use the upper bunk of double-deck beds for a resident's bed;

11) Provide a call bell or intercom system if the provider, entity representative, resident manager or caregiver bedroom is not within hearing distance of each resident bedroom and the system is required by the department;

12) Ensure that members of the household, other than residents, do not share bedrooms with residents; and

13) Ensure a resident does not share a bedroom with a person under eighteen years of age, unless the person is the resident's own child.

[Statutory Authority: RCW 70.128.040. 10-03-064, § 388-76-10685, filed 1/15/10, effective 2/15/10. Statutory Authority: RCW 70.128.040 and chapters 70.128 and 74.34 RCW. 07-21-080, § 388-76-10685, filed 10/16/07, effective 1/1/08.]

388-76-10690
Bedroom usable floor space — In Adult Family Homes after the effective date of this chapter.

1) For the purposes of this section "vestibule" means a small room or hall between an outer door and the main part of the resident bedroom.

2) The Adult Family Home must ensure each resident bedroom has a minimum usable floor space as follows, excluding the floor space for toilet rooms, closets, lockers, wardrobes and vestibules:

   a) Single occupancy bedrooms with at least eighty square feet; and

   b) Double occupancy bedrooms with at least one-hundred twenty square feet.

[Statutory Authority: RCW 70.128.040 and chapters 70.128 and 74.34 RCW. 07-21-080. § 388-76-10690, filed 10/16/07, effective 1/1/08.]

388-76-10695
Building codes — Structural requirements.

1) For single family dwellings used as an Adult Family Home after July 1, 2007, the home must ensure the building meets the requirements of WAC 51-51-0325 Section R325 if the building is:

   a) New; or

   b) An existing building converted for use as an Adult Family Home.

2) For buildings licensed as a home before July 1, 2007, the requirement of subsection (1) of this section does not apply if:

   a) The building sells or transfers to a new owner; and

b) The new owner takes possession of the building before the issuance of the license.

3) The home must ensure that every area used by residents:

a) Has direct access to at least one exit which does not pass through other areas such as a room or garage subject to being locked or blocked from the opposite side; and

b) Is not accessible only by or with the use of a:

i) Ladder;

ii) Folding stairs; or

iii) Trap door.

[Statutory Authority: RCW 70.128.040 and chapters 70.128 and 74.34 RCW. 07-21-080, § 388-76-10695, filed 10/16/07, effective 1/1/08.]

388-76-10700
Building official — Inspection and approval.

The Adult Family Home must have the building inspected and approved for use as an Adult Family Home by the local building official:

1) Before licensing; and

2) After any construction changes that:

a) Affect resident's ability to exit the home; or

b) Change, add or modify a resident's bedroom.

[Statutory Authority: RCW 70.128.040 and chapters 70.128 and 74.34 RCW. 07-21-080, § 388-76-10700, filed 10/16/07, effective 1/1/08.]

388-76-10705
Common use areas.

1) For the purposes of this section, common use areas:

   a) Are areas and rooms of the Adult Family Home that residents use each day for tasks such as eating, visiting, and leisure activities; and

   b) Include but are not limited to dining and eating rooms, living and family rooms, and any entertainment and recreation areas.

2) The Adult Family Home must ensure common use areas are:

   a) Homelike, with furnishings that each resident may use;

   b) Large enough for all residents to use at the same time; and

   c) Not used as bedrooms or sleeping areas.

[Statutory Authority: RCW 70.128.040 and chapters 70.128 and 74.34 RCW. 07-21-080, § 388-76-10705, filed 10/16/07, effective 1/1/08.]

388-76-10710
Construction and remodeling
— Relocation of residents.

Before moving all residents out of the Adult Family Home for construction or remodeling, the home must:

1) Notify the residents of the move date and the resident's options consistent with chapter 70.129 RCW;

2) Notify the department at least thirty days before the anticipated move, including:

   a) The location to which the residents will be moved;

   b) The home's plans for providing and ensuring care and services during the relocation;

   c) The home's plans for returning residents to the building; and

   d) The projected time frame for completing the construction or remodeling.

3) Obtain the department's approval of the relocation plans before moving the residents.

[Statutory Authority: RCW 70.128.040 and chapters 70.128 and 74.34 RCW. 07-21-080, § 388-76-10710, filed 10/16/07, effective 1/1/08.]

388-76-10715
Doors — Ability to open.

The Adult Family Home must ensure:

1) Every bedroom and bathroom door opens from the inside and outside;

2) Every closet door opens from the inside and outside; and

3) All exit doors leading to the outside will open from the inside without a key or any special knowledge or effort by residents.

[Statutory Authority: RCW 70.128.040 and chapters 70.128 and 74.34 RCW. 07-21-080, § 388-76-10715, filed 10/16/07, effective 1/1/08.]

388-76-10720
Electronic monitoring equipment
— Audio monitoring and video monitoring.

1) Except as provided in this section or in WAC 388-76-10725, the Adult Family Home must not use the following in the home:

   a) Audio monitoring equipment; or

   b) Video monitoring equipment if it includes an audio component.

2) The home may video monitor and video record activities in the home, without an audio component, only in the following areas:

a) Entrances and exits if the cameras are:

   i) Focused only on the entrance or exit doorways; and

   ii) Not focused on areas where residents gather.

b) Outdoor areas not commonly used by residents; and

c) Designated smoking areas, subject to the following conditions:

   i) Residents are assessed as needing supervision for smoking;

   ii) A staff person watches the video monitor at any time the area is used by such residents;

   iii) The video camera is clearly visible;

   iv) The video monitor is not viewable by general public; and

   v) The home notifies all residents in writing of the video monitoring equipment.

[Statutory Authority: RCW 70.128.040. 09-03-029, § 388-76-10720, filed 1/12/09, effective 2/12/09. Statutory Authority: RCW 70.128.040 and chapters 70.128 and 74.34 RCW. 07-21-080, § 388-76-10720, filed 10/16/07, effective 1/1/08.]

388-76-10725
Electronic monitoring equipment
— Resident requested use.

1) The Adult Family Home must not use audio or video monitoring equipment to monitor any resident unless:

   a) The resident has requested the monitoring; and

   b) The monitoring is only used in the sleeping room of the resident who requested the monitoring.

2) If the resident requests audio or video monitoring, before any electronic monitoring occurs the home must ensure:

   a) That the electronic monitoring does not violate chapter 9.73 RCW;

   b) The resident has identified a threat to the resident's health, safety or personal property;

   c) The resident's roommate has provided written consent to electronic monitoring, if the resident has a roommate; and

   d) The resident and the home have agreed upon a specific duration for the electronic monitoring documented in writing.

3) The home must:

   a) Reevaluate the need for the electronic monitoring with the resident at least quarterly; and

   b) Have each reevaluation in writing signed and dated by the resident.

4) The home must immediately stop electronic monitoring if the:

   a) Resident no longer wants electronic monitoring;

   b) Roommate objects or withdraws the consent to the electronic monitoring, or

   c) Resident becomes unable to give consent.

5) For the purposes of consenting to video electronic monitoring, without an audio component, the term "resident" includes the resident's decision maker.

6) For the purposes of consenting to audio electronic monitoring, the term "resident includes only:

   a) The resident residing in the home; or

   b) The resident's court-appointed guardian or attorney-in-fact who has obtained a court order specifically authorizing the court-appointed guardian or attorney-in-fact to consent to audio electronic monitoring of the resident.

7) If the resident's decision maker consents to audio electronic monitoring as specified in subsection (6) above, the home must maintain a copy of the court order authorizing such consent in the resident's record.

[Statutory Authority: RCW 70.128.040. 09-03-029, § 388-76-10725, filed 1/12/09, effective 2/12/09. Statutory Authority: RCW 70.128.040 and chapters 70.128 and 74.34 RCW. 07-21-080, § 388-76-10725, filed 10/16/07, effective 1/1/08.]

388-76-10730
Grab bars and hand rails.

1) The Adult Family Home must install grab bars or hand rails to meet the needs of each resident.

2) At a minimum, grab bars must be installed and securely fastened in:

   a) Bathing facilities such as tubs and showers; and

   b) Next to toilets, if needed by any resident.

3) If needed by any resident, hand rails must be installed and conveniently located on:

   a) A step or steps; and

   b) Ramps.

[Statutory Authority: RCW 70.128.040 and chapters 70.128 and 74.34 RCW. 07-21-080, § 388-76-10730, filed 10/16/07, effective 1/1/08.]

388-76-10735
Kitchen facilities.

1) The Adult Family Home must ensure the kitchen facilities include adequate space for:

   a) Food handling;

b) Preparation; and

c) Food storage.

2) The home must keep the kitchen and equipment in a clean and sanitary manner.

[Statutory Authority: RCW 70.128.040 and chapters 70.128 and 74.34 RCW. 07-21-080, § 388-76-10735, filed 10/16/07, effective 1/1/08.]

388-76-10740
Lighting.

The Adult Family Home must provide:

1) Adequate light fixtures for each task a resident or staff does; and

2) Emergency lighting, such as working flashlights for staff and residents that are readily accessible.

[Statutory Authority: RCW 70.128.040 and chapters 70.128 and 74.34 RCW. 07-21-080, § 388-76-10740, filed 10/16/07, effective 1/1/08.]

388-76-10745
Local codes and ordinances.

The Adult Family Home must:

1) Meet all applicable local licensing, zoning, building

and housing codes as they pertain to a single family dwelling;

2) Meet state and local fire safety regulations as they pertain to a single family dwelling; and

3) Check with local authorities to ensure the home meets all local codes and ordinances.

[Statutory Authority: RCW 70.128.040 and chapters 70.128 and 74.34 RCW. 07-21-080, § 388-76-10745, filed 10/16/07, effective 1/1/08.]

388-76-10750
Safety and maintenance.

The Adult Family Home must:

1) Keep the home both internally and externally in good repair and condition with a safe, comfortable, sanitary, homelike environment that is free of hazards;

2) Ensure that there is existing outdoor space that is safe and usable for residents;

3) Provide clean, functioning, safe, adequate household items and furnishings to meet the needs of each resident;

4) Provide safe and functioning systems for:

    a) Heating;

    b) Cooling, which may include air circulating fans;

   c) Hot and cold water;

   d) Electricity;

   e) Plumbing;

   f) Garbage disposal;

   g) Sewage;

   h) Cooking;

   i) Laundry;

   j) Artificial and natural light;

   k) Ventilation; and

   l) Any other feature of the home.

5) Ensure water temperature does not exceed one hundred twenty degrees Fahrenheit at all fixtures used by or accessible to residents, such as:

   a) Tubs;

   b) Showers; and

   c) Sinks.

6) Provide storage for toxic substances, poisons, and other hazardous materials that is only accessible to residents under direct supervision, unless the resident is assessed for and the negotiated care plan indicates it is safe for the resident to use the materials unsupervised;

7) Provide rapid access for all staff to any bedroom,

toilet room, shower room, closet, other room occupied by each resident;

8) Keep all firearms locked and accessible only to authorized persons; and

9) Keep the home free from:

   a) Rodents;

   b) Flies;

   c) Cockroaches, and

   d) Other vermin.

[Statutory Authority: RCW 70.128.040. 10-03-064, § 388-76-10750, filed 1/15/10, effective 2/15/10. Statutory Authority: RCW 70.128.040 and chapters 70.128 and 74.34 RCW. 07-21-080, § 388-76-10750, filed 10/16/07, effective 1/1/08.]

388-76-10755
Sewage and liquid wastes.

The Adult Family Home must ensure sewage and liquid wastes are discharged into:

1) A public sewer system; or

2) An independent sewage system approved by the local health authority.

[Statutory Authority: RCW 70.128.040 and chapters 70.128 and 74.34 RCW. 07-21-080, § 388-76-10755, filed 10/16/07, effective 1/1/08.]

388-76-10760
Site.

The Adult Family Home must ensure the home:

1) Is on a well drained site free from:

   a) Hazardous conditions;

   b) Excessive noise;

   c) Dust; and

   d) Smoke or odors.

2) Has a road accessible at all times to emergency vehicles.

[Statutory Authority: RCW 70.128.040 and chapters 70.128 and 74.34 RCW. 07-21-080, § 388-76-10760, filed 10/16/07, effective 1/1/08.]

388-76-10765
Storage.

The Adult Family Home must:

1) Supply each resident with adequate and reasonable storage space for:

   a) Clothing;

   b) Personal possessions; and

    c)   Upon request, lockable container or storage space for small items, unless the:

         i)   Resident has a private room; and

         ii) The resident room can be locked by the resident.

2)   Provide locked storage for all prescribed and over-the-counter medications as per WAC 388-76-10485.

[Statutory Authority: RCW 70.128.040 and chapters 70.128 and 74.34 RCW. 07-21-080, § 388-76-10765, filed 10/16/07, effective 1/1/08.]

388-76-10770
Telephones.

The Adult Family Home must provide:

1)   At least one working nonpay telephone in the home;

2)   Residents reasonable access to the telephone; and

3)   Privacy for the resident when making or receiving calls.

[Statutory Authority: RCW 70.128.040 and chapters 70.128 and 74.34 RCW. 07-21-080, § 388-76-10770, filed 10/16/07, effective 1/1/08.]

388-76-10775
Temperature and ventilation.

The Adult Family Home must:

1) Ensure that the maximum and minimum temperature of any room used by a resident is comfortable for the resident and does not compromise the resident's health and safety.

2) At a minimum, keep room temperature at:

   a) Sixty-eight degrees Fahrenheit or more during waking hours; and

   b) Sixty degrees Fahrenheit or more during sleeping hours.

3) Provide ventilation in the home to ensure the health and comfort of each resident is met.

[Statutory Authority: RCW 70.128.040. 09-03-029, § 388-76-10775, filed 1/12/09, effective 2/12/09. Statutory Authority: RCW 70.128.040 and chapters 70.128 and 74.34 RCW. 07-21-080, § 388-76-10775, filed 10/16/07, effective 1/1/08.]

388-76-10780
Toilets and bathing facilities.

1) The Adult Family Home must ensure the home has toilets and bathing facilities that provide each resident with privacy and include:

   a) One indoor flush toilet for each five persons

including residents and household members in the home; and

b) Sinks with hot and cold running water.

2) Homes licensed after July 1, 2007, must ensure each resident has access to a toilet, shower or tub without going through another resident's room.

[Statutory Authority: RCW 70.128.040 and chapters 70.128 and 74.34 RCW. 07-21-080, § 388-76-10780, filed 10/16/07, effective 1/1/08.]

388-76-10783
Water hazards and bodies of water — Resident safety.

The Adult Family Home must protect each resident:

1) From risks associated with water hazards or bodies of water of any depth at the home; and

2) When accompanying or escorting the resident at other locations where there are water hazards or bodies of water of any depth.

[Statutory Authority: RCW 70.128.040. 09-03-030, § 388-76-10783, filed 1/12/09, effective 2/12/09.]

388-76-10784
Water hazards
— Fences, gates and alarms.

For any Adult Family Home newly licensed after July 1, 2007 or any currently licensed Adult Family Home that adds or modifies a new or existing water hazard after July 1, 2007 must:

1) Comply with this section and the requirements of the:

   a) International Residential Code (IRC); and

   b) Washington state amendments to the International Residential Code (IRC).

2) Enclose water hazards over twenty four inches deep with:

   a) Fences and gates at least forty-eight inches high; and

   b) Audible alarms when doors, screens, and gates that directly lead to or surround the water hazard, are opened.

[Statutory Authority: RCW 70.128.040. 09-03-030, § 388-76-10784, filed 1/12/09, effective 2/12/09.]

388-76-10790
Water supply.

The Adult Family Home must:

1) Obtain local health authority approval to use a private water supply;

2) Provide a clean and healthy drinking water supply for the home; and

3) Label any nonpotable water to avoid use as a drinking water source.

[Statutory Authority: RCW 70.128.040 and chapters 70.128 and 74.34 RCW. 07-21-080, § 388-76-10790, filed 10/16/07, effective 1/1/08.]

388-76-10795
Windows.

1) The Adult Family Home must ensure the sill height of the bedroom window is not more than forty-four inches above the floor.

2) For homes licensed after July 1, 2007, the department will not approve alternatives to the sill height requirement such as step(s), raised platform(s) or other devices placed by or under the window openings.

3) The bedroom window must have the following:

   a) A minimum opening area of 5.7 square feet except a grade level floor window openings may have a minimum clear opening of 5.0 square feet;

b) A minimum opening height of twenty-four inches; and

c) A minimum opening width of twenty inches.

4) The home must ensure the bedroom window can be opened from inside the room without keys or tools.

5) When resident bedroom windows are fitted with storm windows, the home must equip the storm windows with release mechanisms that:

a) Easily open from the inside; and

b) Do not require a key or special knowledge or effort to open.

6) The home must ensure that each basement and each resident bedroom window, that meets the requirements of subsection (1), (2) and (3) of this section, are kept free from obstructions that might block or interfere with access for emergency escape or rescue.

[Statutory Authority: RCW 70.128.040 and chapters 70.128 and 74.34 RCW. 07-21-080, § 388-76-10795, filed 10/16/07, effective 1/1/08.]

388-76-10800

Adult Family Home located outside of public fire protection.

If the Adult Family Home is located in an area without public fire protection, the home must have written verification of adequate fire protection from the fire authority.

[Statutory Authority: RCW 70.128.040 and chapters 70.128 and 74.34 RCW. 07-21-080, § 388-76-10800, filed 10/16/07, effective 1/1/08.]

388-76-10805
Automatic smoke detectors.

The Adult Family Home must ensure approved automatic smoke detectors are:

1) Installed, at a minimum, in the following locations:

   a) Every bedroom used by a resident;

   b) In proximity to the area where the resident or Adult Family Home staff sleeps; and

   c) On every level of a multilevel home.

2) Installed in a manner so that the fire warning is heard in all parts of the home upon activation of a single detector; and

3) Kept in working condition at all times.

[Statutory Authority: RCW 70.128.040 and chapters 70.128 and 74.34 RCW. 07-21-080, § 388-76-10805, filed 10/16/07, effective 1/1/08.]

388-76-10810
Fire extinguishers.

1) The Adult Family Home must have an approved five pound 2A:10B-C rated fire extinguisher on each floor of the home.

2) The home must ensure the fire extinguishers are:

   a) Installed according to manufacturer recommendations;

   b) Inspected and serviced annually;

   c) In proper working order; and

   d) Readily available for use at all times.

3) If required by the local fire authority, the home must provide different fire extinguishers in place of the fire extinguishers required in subsection (1) of this section.

[Statutory Authority: RCW 70.128.040. 08-09-028, § 388-76-10810, filed 4/8/08, effective 5/9/08. Statutory Authority: RCW 70.128.040 and chapters 70.128 and 74.34 RCW. 07-21-080, § 388-76-10810, filed 10/16/07, effective 1/1/08.]

About the Author

John P Neff, CBO, is a retired Building Official, Fire Marshal and Capital Projects Manager with 32+ years of experience in local government performing building code administration.

John is also a former carpenter; former City Council Member; former Board Member of the Washington Association of Building Officials, International Conference of Building Officials/International Code Council and International Accreditation Service; former member and Chair of the WA State Building Code Council and member of the World Organization of Building Officials.

John has long been active in code development and teaching others the various codes and how to best administer them for the benefit of the public.

Much more importantly than any of the above, however, is that John has always had a very warm spot in his heart for the elderly. From the early days of visiting with the "old guys" at the Chelan, WA Post Office when he and his

Grandpa Wooton would go for the mail; to not getting his paper route collecting done, because he talked too long with the retired folks; to working in a nursing home, to helping his own and his wife's parents all out of this world into the next, the care of the elderly has been very, very important.

It is hoped this feeling of caring, respect and retaining the dignity in the lives of the elderly who reside in care facilities has come through in this book. If so, it is a success.